A Dog Path

Level 3 – Yellow

Helpful Hints for Reading at Home

The graphemes (written letters) and phonemes (units of sound) used throughout this series are aligned with Letters and Sounds. This offers a consistent approach to learning, whether reading at home or in the classroom.

HERE IS A LIST OF PHONEMES FOR THIS PHASE OF LEARNING. AN EXAMPLE OF THE PRONUNCIATION CAN BE FOUND IN BRACKETS.

Phase 3			
j (jug)	v (van)	w (wet)	x (fox)
y (yellow)	z (zoo)	zz (buzz)	qu (quick)
ch (chip)	sh (shop)	th (thin/then)	ng (ring)
ai (rain)	ee (feet)	igh (night)	oa (boat)
oo (boot/look)	ar (farm)	or (for)	ur (hurt)
ow (cow)	oi (coin)	ear (dear)	air (fair)
ure (sure)	er (corner)		

HERE ARE SOME WORDS WHICH YOUR CHILD MAY FIND TRICKY.

Phase 3 Tricky Words			
he	you	she	they
we	all	me	are
be	my	was	her

TOP TIPS FOR HELPING YOUR CHILD TO READ:

- Allow children time to break down unfamiliar words into units of sound and then encourage children to string these sounds together to create the word.

- Encourage your child to point out any focus phonics when they are used.

- Read through the book more than once to grow confidence.

- Ask simple questions about the text to assess understanding.

- Encourage children to use illustrations as prompts.

This book focuses on /th/ and is a Yellow level 3 book band.

Can you say this sound and draw it with your finger?

Can they go on this path with a dog?
They can.

They go on the path with the dog.

They let the dog run and pass them.

The dog has to go to the loo.

They pick it up and let it go in the bin.

This bit is wet. Will the dog run in it?

He will. The wet path is fun to run on.

Get the dog in the bath!

©2023 **BookLife Publishing Ltd.**
King's Lynn, Norfolk, PE30 4LS, UK

ISBN 978–1–80505–117–6

All rights reserved. Printed in China.
A catalogue record for this book is available from the British Library.

A Dog Path
Written by Charis Mather
Designed by Jasmine Pointer

An Introduction to BookLife Readers...

Our Readers have been specifically created in line with the London Institute of Education's approach to book banding and are phonetically decodable and ordered to support each phase of Letters and Sounds.

Each book has been created to provide the best possible reading and learning experience. Our aim is to share our love of books with children, providing both emerging readers and prolific page-turners with beautiful books that are guaranteed to provoke interest and learning, regardless of ability.

BOOK BAND GRADED using the Institute of Education's approach to levelling.

PHONETICALLY DECODABLE supporting each phase of Letters and Sounds.

EXERCISES AND QUESTIONS to offer reinforcement and to ascertain comprehension.

CLEAR DESIGN to inspire and provoke engagement, providing the reader with clear visual representations of each non-fiction topic.

AUTHOR INSIGHT:
CHARIS MATHER

Charis Mather is a children's author at BookLife Publishing who has a love for reading and writing. Her studies in linguistics and experiences working with young readers have given her a knack for writing material that suits a range of ages and skill levels. Charis is passionate about producing books that emphasise the fun in reading and is convinced that no matter how much you already know, there is always something new to learn.

PHASE 3 /th/

This book focuses on /th/ and is a Yellow level 3 book band.

Image Credits Images are courtesy of Shutterstock.com. With thanks to Getty Images, Thinkstock Photo and iStockphoto. Cover – Parilov, Chinch, eatcute. 4–5 – Nick Beer, Monkey Business Images. 6–7 – Hollysdogs, sanjagrujic. 8–9 – Helena56, SarahBavaria. 10–11 – Alex Zotov, Jaromir Chalabala.

BookLife Non-Fiction Readers

Caterpillar to Butterfly
9781839278938

Chinese New Year
9781839278921

Dig a Pit
9781839278945

Tap the Puck
9781839278952

Pets
9781839278976

Picnic
9781839278969

Queens and Kings
9781839278990

Vets
9781839278983

At the Fun Fair
9781839279010

Look Up!
9781839279003

At the Shop
9781839279027

The Fixer's Lesson on: Screws
9781839279034

Stay Safe Online
9781839279058

Habitats
9781839279041

EXPLORE A WORLD OF NON-FICTION WITH OUR DECODABLE READER RANGE

MORE COMING SOON

BookLife PUBLISHING

BookLife Readers

The BookLife Readers begin with the very basics of **phonetically decodable reading**. Starting with the earliest step of **CVC** words–words comprising of a consonant, a vowel and a consonant–and building on this combination slowly, the reader follows a prescribed format taken directly from the recognised **Letters and Sounds** educational document.

By aligning our books with Letters and Sounds, we offer our readers a consistent approach to learning, whether at home or in the classroom. Our Readers each feature a focus sound to help learners practice reading specific graphemes. These focus sounds will feature more heavily in that title than in others in the same band. The illustrations and photographs guide the reader, helping to deliver reading progression through the scheme in a colourful and exciting way. As a reader moves through the book band levels, the page numbers, levels of repetition and sentence structure complexity all advance at a rate which encourages development without halting enjoyment.

To find out more about this exciting reading scheme, visit **www.booklife.co.uk**